Praying in Silence
of Heart

Also available from GIA Publications, Inc.
by Brother Roger:

The Sources of Taizé (G-5363)

Peace of Heart in All Things: Meditations for Each Day of the Year
(G-6513)

God Is Love Alone (G-6259)

Glimmers of Happiness (G-7078)

Other Taizé titles:

A Universal Heart: The Life and Vision of Brother Roger of Taizé
by Kathryn Spink (G-6773)

Prayer for Each Day (G-4918)

Seeds of Trust: Reflecting on the Bible in Silence and Song
(G-6719)

Seek and You Will Find:
Questions on the Christian Faith and the Bible
(G-6879)

Taizé: A Meaning to Life by Oliver Clément (G-4755)

Praying in Silence of Heart
One Hundred Prayers

Brother Roger of Taizé

GIA Publications, Inc.
Chicago

ISBN: 978-1-57999-658-1
(USA, Canada, and USA dependencies)

G-7077
Copyright © 2007 Ateliers et Presses de Taizé. Published and distributed in North America by GIA Publications, Inc.

This compilation originally published in French as *Prier dans le silence du cœur: cent prières*, copyright © Ateliers et Presses de Taizé, F-71250 Taizé–Communauté, France, 2005. English translation copyright © Ateliers et Presses de Taizé, F-71250 Taizé–Communauté, France, 2005.

Cover photo credit S. Leutenegger

GIA Publications, Inc.
7404 S. Mason Ave., Chicago, IL 60638
www.giamusic.com

Printed in the U.S.A.

Contents

Nothing
Is More Responsible
than Praying

Personal prayer is always going to remain simple. Do we believe that many words are needed in praying? No. There are times when just a few words, often awkward ones, are quite enough for us to be able to entrust everything to God, our fears and our hopes.

As we abandon ourselves to the Holy Spirit, we find a path leading from anxiety to trust.

In prayer, we are enabled to sense that we are never alone: the Holy Spirit sustains within us a communion with God, not for just one moment, but on into that life that has no end.

Yes, the Holy Spirit kindles within us a light. No matter how pale it seems, it awakens in our souls the desire for God. And that simple desire for God is already prayer.

Praying does not remove us from the world's preoccupations. On the contrary, nothing is more responsible than praying: the more we live a very simple, very humble prayer, the more we are brought to love and to express that by our lives.

Holy Spirit,
enable us to bring peace
into places of opposition,
and to make visible
by our lives
a reflection of God's compassion.
Yes, enable us to love
and to express it by our lives.

Jesus, our peace,
by your Gospel
you call us to be very simple,
very humble.
You give growth within us
to an infinite gratitude
for your constant presence
in our hearts.

God of consolation,
even when we feel nothing
of your presence,
still, you are there.
Your presence is invisible
but your Holy Spirit
is always within us.

Holy Spirit,
you fill the universe,
and you bring within the reach
of our fragile humanity
these Gospel values:
goodness of heart, forgiveness,
compassion.

God of every human being,
when we simply desire
to welcome your love,
a flame rises up little by little
deep in our souls.
Very fragile though it be,
it always keeps burning.

Jesus, our hope,
in you we find the consolation
with which God comes to flood
     our lives,
and we understand that,
in prayer,
we can bring everything to you,
entrust everything to you.

Holy Spirit,
you have a call for every one of us.
So come, prepare our hearts
to discover what it is
that you expect of each of us.

God of compassion,
disconcerted by the incomprehensible
suffering of the innocent,
we pray for those
who are experiencing times
of trial.
Inspire the hearts of those
who seek the peace
that is so indispensable
for the whole human family.

Holy Spirit,
in you we are offered
a way of discovering this amazing
reality:
God does not wish suffering
or distress for people;
he never creates fear or anguish
in us.
God can only love us.

God of consolation,
you burden yourself with our
   burdens
so that we can move forward
at every moment,
from anxiety toward trust,
from shadows toward light.

Jesus, peace of our hearts,
in our nights
as in our days,
in the hours of darkness
as in those of bright light,
you knock at our doors
and await our response.

Holy Spirit,
mystery of a presence,
you enfold us with your peace
that comes to touch
our inward-most heart,
bringing us a breath of life.

God, you love us,
so no matter how poor our prayer
we seek you with confidence.
Your love burrows a way
through our hesitations
and even through our doubts.

Jesus, our peace,
you call us to follow you
throughout our whole lives.
So, with humble trust,
we come to realize
that you are inviting us to
    welcome you
again and again, forever.

Holy Spirit,
even when our words
hardly manage to express
our longing
for a communion with you,
your invisible presence
dwells within each one,
and so a joy may be offered us.

God of merciful compassion,
enable us to find ways
of waiting for you in prayer
and of welcoming the loving gaze
with which you behold each
one's life.

Jesus, our hearts' joy,
you pour out within us the
    Holy Spirit.
He comes to renew trust
deep inside us.
Through him we understand
that the simple longing for God
restores our souls to life.

Holy Spirit, comforter,
come and breathe on the anxieties
that are capable of keeping us
far from you.
And so enable us to discover
the sources of trust
that are already there in our
    inmost hearts.

God of compassion,
by the Gospel
we can sense
that you love us
even in our most secret solitudes.
Happy those who abandon
    themselves to you
with trusting hearts.

Jesus, our trust,
within us you come
bearing a flame.
Feeble though it may be,
it is enough to sustain in our hearts
the desire for God.

Holy Spirit,
by your constant presence in us
you guide us
to give our lives in love.
And even if we sometimes
forget you,
you bestow on us a joy.

Jesus of merciful compassion,
overwhelmed with trials,
you threatened no one,
you forgave.
We too wish to know how
    to forgive
remaining
very simple of heart.

To Whom Should We Go,
Other than You?

For as long as we can go back in history, vast numbers of believers have known that, in prayer, God brings a light, a life within.

Long before Christ, one believer prayed: "My soul longs for you by night, Lord; deep within me, my spirit seeks you."

A desire for a communion with God has lain within the human heart from endless ages of time. The mystery of that communion touches the most inward, the very inmost depths of our being.

So we can say to Christ: "To whom should we go, other than you? You have the words that bring our souls to life."

Christ of compassion,
you welcome us
with our gifts and our frailties.
And by the Holy Spirit
you liberate,
you forgive,
you guide us to the point where
we give our very lives in love.

God of all loving,
we long to be attentive
when deep within us
your call rings out:
"Onward, and may your soul live!"

Holy Spirit, consoling Spirit,
receive our very simple prayer
as we seek
to entrust everything to you
and to rejoice at what you
    accomplish
in our souls.

Christ Jesus,
give us resolute hearts,
hearts that, in simple prayer,
untiringly seek
to discover a communion
with God.

God of mercy,
the Gospel enables us to grasp
this good news:
no one,
yes, no one is excluded
from your love,
from your forgiveness.

Holy Spirit, inner light,
we would wish never
to choose darkness
but ever to welcome
a light coming from you.

Jesus, our joy,
you call us to follow you,
and we realize that
your Gospel can transform
our hearts and our lives.

God of compassion,
we praise you for the multitudes
of women, men, young people,
who, all over the world,
seek to bear witness
to peace,
to reconciliation,
to communion.

Holy Spirit, consoling Spirit,
when we remain in your presence,
silent, at peace,
that is already prayer.
You understand everything
    about us,
and at times even a simple sigh
can be a prayer.

Jesus, Savior of every life,
as the morning star rises in
   our hearts,
you shed light even on our doubts
and our hesitations.

God, you love
every human person,
and we yearn to live
a communion with you
day by day,
in silence and in love.

Holy Spirit,
filling the universe,
as a breath of silence
you tell each of us:
"Be afraid of nothing.
Deep within you
is the presence of God;
seek and you will find."

Jesus, peace for our hearts,
your Gospel comes to open
    our eyes
to the fullness of your love:
it is forgiveness,
inner light.

God of all loving,
as we seek you with confidence,
we wait
for even our inner contradictions
to open to the presence
of your Holy Spirit.

Holy Spirit,
you do not wish us
to be anxious,
you enfold us with your peace.
It prepares us
to live each day
as a day that belongs to God.

Christ Jesus,
you came into the world,
not to condemn the world
but so that, by the Holy Spirit,
we could live
a communion with God.

God of peace,
although we may be fragile,
we are eager to follow you
along the way that leads us
to love
as you love us.

Holy Spirit,
mystery of a presence,
you say to each of us:
"Why be worried?
One thing alone is necessary:
a heart attentive
to understand
that God loves you
and always forgives you."

Jesus, our hope,
fragile and empty-handed we
    may be,
but we long to understand
that you always shed light
on the way that leads to God.

God of love,
by your Holy Spirit
you are always present.
Your presence is invisible,
but you live in the midst of
    our souls,
even when we do not realize it.

Holy Spirit,
breath of God's loving,
our prayer may be very
humble,
yet by the Gospel
we understand that you are praying
even in the silence
of our hearts.

A Contemplative Way
of Looking

It is not too much, for the human beings that we are, to remain before God in contemplative waiting.

In such prayer, a veil is lifted from what in faith cannot be expressed, and the inexpressible leads to adoration.

God is also present when fervor evaporates, when feelings weaken. We are never deprived of God's compassion. It is not God who is remote from us, but we who are sometimes absent.

With eyes of contemplation, we perceive signs of the Gospel in the simplest events.

They discern Christ's presence in even the most forsaken human being.

They discover throughout the universe the radiant beauty of creation.

Holy Spirit,
always you come to enfold us
in your peace.
And when within us dwells
a joy drawn from the Gospel,
it is capable of bringing us
a breath of life.

God, you love us,
and the contemplation of your
   forgiveness
becomes a ray of goodness
in the humble heart
that entrusts itself to you.

Jesus, peace of our hearts,
you call each of us
to follow you.
To whom should we go,
other than you?
You, Christ, have the words
that give life to our souls.

Praised be the Holy Spirit!
Present in the depths of our souls,
and consuming the hard things
in our lives
by the fire of that presence.

God of peace,
you strive to set within us
a Gospel joy.
It is there, very nearby,
ever renewed by the trusting way
you behold our lives.

Jesus, our hope,
your Gospel enables us
to sense that,
even in dark times,
God wants us to be happy.
And the peace in our hearts
can make life beautiful
for those around us.

Holy Spirit,
filling the universe,
you give growth within each
    one of us
to a life of communion with God.
And there, opening out, spring
    goodness of heart
and a self-forgetting for the sake of
    others.

God of mercy,
you shed an unexpected light
within our souls.
By it we discover that,
while a portion of darkness
may remain in us,
there is above all in everyone
the mystery of your presence.

Jesus Christ,
we seek you as you behold us.
Your looking comes to banish
the pain from our hearts.
Then you say:
"Do not worry;
though I am invisible,
always I am with you."

Holy Spirit,
you open us to a Gospel reality:
love that forgives,
so much so that nothing is
    disastrous
except the loss
of the spirit of merciful love.

God of consolation,
by your Holy Spirit
you come to transfigure our hearts.
In the midst of our very trials
you give growth
to a communion with you.

Jesus, our hearts' joy,
you enable all
who live by your forgiveness
and compassion
to sense the greatest
of all certainties:
wherever there is mercy,
God is there.

God, you love every human
   person.
When we realize
that our love
is forgiveness above all,
our hearts find peace,
and may even be changed.

Christ Jesus,
you have a call for each of us,
as you say:
Come, follow me,
and you will find a resting place
for your heart.

Holy Spirit, consoling Spirit,
with you we discover
that we are never alone
and you sustain within us
a constant communion
with God.

God of all eternity,
we long to seek for you
amidst the silences of prayer
and live by the hope
discovered in the Gospel.

Christ Jesus,
by your Gospel we realize
that what counts above all
is compassion.
Grant us, then,
hearts full of goodness.

Holy Spirit,
when our hearts feel anxious,
you open a way ahead
for each of us:
it means entrusting
our whole life to God.

God of all tenderness,
in you we can discover
the meaning of our existence:
it is to give our lives
on account of Christ and the
Gospel.

Jesus,
in the Gospel you tell us
not to linger
over things that have hurt us.
And your forgiveness becomes a
    miracle
in our lives.

God, as you love us,
we long to go to your living
    springs,
in days of joy
and in days of pain.
There, by your Holy Spirit,
you speak to our hearts.

Holy Spirit,
you are in communion
with each of us,
not for just a moment
but forever, on into the life
that knows no end.

Surrendering Oneself to God

When our personal praying seems poor and our words awkward, we should not stop midway.

Isn't one of our soul's deepest desires to attain a communion with God?

Three centuries after Christ, an African Christian named Augustine wrote: "A desire calling on God is already prayer. If you would pray without ceasing, never stop desiring. . . ."

A great simplicity of heart underlies and sustains a contemplative prayer. That allows us to surrender ourselves to God, letting ourselves be borne toward him.

This process of self-surrender may be sustained by simple songs, repeated over and over, such as: "My soul finds rest in God alone."

While we are working and while we are resting, such songs continue within our hearts.

In a life of communion of this kind, God, who remains invisible, will not necessarily address us in language that can be translated into human words. Above all, God speaks by silent intuitions.

In prayer, silence seems to be nothing special. Yet in that silence, the Holy Spirit may enable us to welcome God's joy as it comes to touch the depths of the soul.

Christ Jesus,
Savior of every life,
you suffer with all
who experience hardships,
and you always welcome
any who entrust to you
their own burdens.

Breath of the love of God,
Holy Spirit,
at times we are quite taken aback
to discover how close you are
to us.
To each one you say:
surrender yourself very simply
in God; your little faith is enough.

God of peace,
you love and you seek out
every one of us.
You consider each human being
with an infinite tenderness
and deep compassion.

Jesus, we long to live
by those words
you speak to us in the Gospel:
"My peace I leave you,
let not your heart
be troubled anymore."

Holy Spirit,
enable us to turn toward you
at every moment.
We so often forget
that you are dwelling in us,
that you are praying in us,
that you are loving in us.
Your presence in us
is trust and constant forgiveness.

Merciful God,
in the footsteps of the apostles
and of the Virgin Mary,
you are preparing us
to abandon ourselves in you,
in trust and in love.

Jesus, hope of our hearts,
you dwell in us,
and by your Gospel
you tell each one of us:
"Fear not, I am with you."

Holy Spirit,
mystery of a presence,
you always come to us.
You remain
in the very depths of our souls,
and you awaken within us the
    expectation
of a communion with you.

God of all loving,
for each of us you wish
a Gospel joy.
And when we experience trials,
a way forward remains open,
that of abandoning ourselves
in you.

Christ,
you penetrate our inmost depths,
and there you perceive an
    expectation.
You know that, without having
    seen you
we love you,
and still without seeing you,
we give you our trust.

Holy Spirit, inner light,
you shine on the happy days
as on the troubled times
of our lives.
And when the light seems to grow
dim,
your presence remains.

God of all eternity,
you love each one of us
without exception
and in your constant forgiveness
we discover peace of heart.

Jesus of compassionate mercy,
you enable us to transmit
to those around us
a flame of hope
by the trust of our hearts.

Holy Spirit, Comforter,
to us, the humble of the Gospel,
you have entrusted a mystery of
	hope.
Even when we are unaware of it,
it is there
sustaining our trust.

God of compassion,
as we hearken to your Holy Spirit,
we long to remain
trusting enough
to be able to abandon ourselves to
    you
in every situation.

Jesus, our peace,
with our very little faith,
we long to be attentive to you
as you tell us:
"Turn to God,
and put your trust
in the Gospel."

Holy Spirit,
breath of the love of Christ,
you are always present;
deep in our souls
you lay the trust of faith.

God of peace,
by your Holy Spirit
you enable us to cross
the deserts of the heart
and, by your forgiveness,
you scatter our faults
like the morning mist.

Christ Jesus,
born poor among the poor,
you are God's humility,
and you come, not to judge,
but to open a way
of communion with God.

God, you love every human
  person.
When we surrender ourselves to
  you,
we come to understand that
even what pains our heart
is made bright by the Holy Spirit.

Jesus, our trust,
we long to love you
wholeheartedly.
Grant us the daring we need
to keep renewing
over and over again
the gift of our lives.

Holy Spirit,
open us to trust
and to simplicity of heart,
so we can forget ourselves
and abandon ourselves in you.

He Accompanies Us

On the evening of Easter day, Jesus was accompanying two of his disciples on their way to the village of Emmaus. At that moment, they did not realize that he was walking beside them.

We too experience periods when we are unable to sense that Christ, by the Holy Spirit, is there close by us.

Tirelessly he accompanies us. He sheds unexpected light into our souls. Then we discover that, while a certain darkness may remain within us, there is above all else in each one the mystery of his presence.

Let us try to be certain of one thing! Of what? Christ tells each one: "I love you with a love that will never end. I shall never leave you. By the Holy Spirit, I shall always be with you."

For Christmas

God of peace,
at Christmas we discover,
following in the footsteps of the
	Virgin Mary,
that one of the Gospel's pure joys
is advancing toward a simplicity
of heart and of life.
With the little we have,
we long to welcome you
in silence and in love.

For the Epiphany

God of love,
in our darkness
your presence comes to kindle
an inner flame.
On the day of the Epiphany,
we are able to realize that
it is not ourselves who create
that source of light,
but your Holy Spirit,
who dwells deep within us.

For Palm Sunday

Christ Jesus,
like your disciples on Palm Sunday
we too need a joy
to help prepare us to bear,
with you, our own cross.
You tell each of us:
do not be afraid,
take the risk of following me
again and again forever.

For Holy Thursday

God of compassion,
our hearts and minds are like
dry ground thirsting for you.
Then you spread upon us your
    Spirit:
peace of the Eucharist
that brings us alive.

For Good Friday

Holy Spirit,
by your presence within us
today you prepare us
to perceive God's compassion
and to understand that God
can only give his love.

For Holy Saturday

God of all eternity,
even when all within us
is silence,
our hearts speak to you,
praying,
and we abandon ourselves in you.

For Easter

Christ Jesus,
like some of your disciples,
we sometimes find ourselves
struggling to understand
your risen presence.
But by your Holy Spirit
you live in us,
and to each one you say:
"Come, follow me; I have opened
    for you
a way of life."

For Pentecost

Christ Jesus,
in your Gospel
you assure us:
I will never leave you all alone,
I will send you the Holy Spirit
to be support and comfort,
to enable you
to be in communion with God
day after day.

For the Transfiguration of Christ (August 6)

Holy Spirit,
you know our frailties,
but you come to transfigure our
    hearts,
so that our very darkness itself
can become
inner light.

For All Saints' Day (November 1)

God of loving mercy,
in the footsteps of the saints,
all the witnesses to Christ
since the apostles and the
   Virgin Mary
until today,
you are calling us
to be bearers of peace,
of trust and of joy
for those around us.

For the Death of Someone Dear

Christ of compassion,
you enable us
to be in communion
with those who have gone
   before us,
who can remain so close to us.
They already behold the invisible.
In their footsteps,
you prepare us to welcome
a gleam of your brightness.

For the Birth of a Child

God of all tenderness,
you come and make of us
the humble of the Gospel.
We are so eager to understand
that the best within us
is built up by means of
a very simple trust,
which even a child can achieve.

For a Baptism

God, you love us.
Baptized in the Holy Spirit,
we have forever welcomed Christ.
And to each one of us you say:
"You are unique to me;
in you I find my joy."